TROLLS

Compiled and Illustrated
by
Doug Cushman

Platt & Munk, Publishers/New York
A Division of Grosset & Dunlap

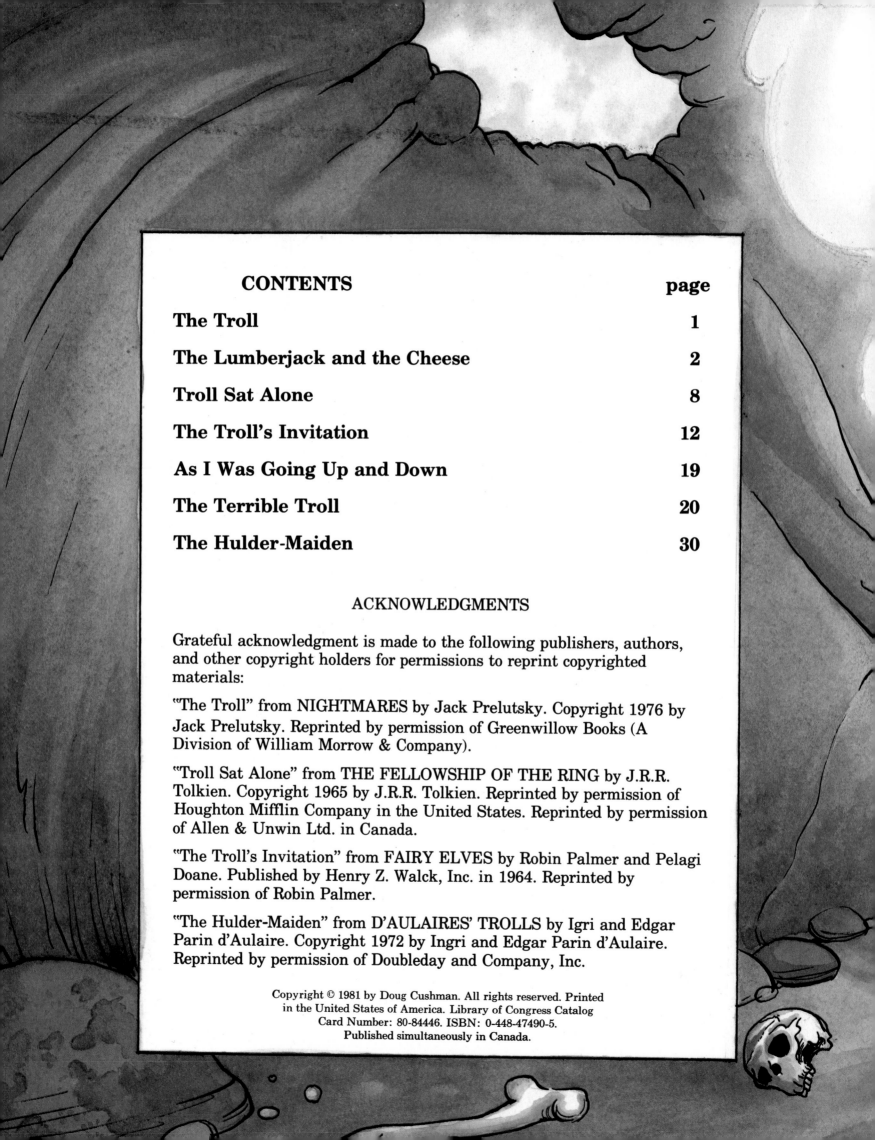

CONTENTS

ACKNOWLEDGMENTS

Grateful acknowledgment is made to the following publishers, authors, and other copyright holders for permissions to reprint copyrighted materials:

"The Troll" from NIGHTMARES by Jack Prelutsky. Copyright 1976 by Jack Prelutsky. Reprinted by permission of Greenwillow Books (A Division of William Morrow & Company).

"Troll Sat Alone" from THE FELLOWSHIP OF THE RING by J.R.R. Tolkien. Copyright 1965 by J.R.R. Tolkien. Reprinted by permission of Houghton Mifflin Company in the United States. Reprinted by permission of Allen & Unwin Ltd. in Canada.

"The Troll's Invitation" from FAIRY ELVES by Robin Palmer and Pelagi Doane. Published by Henry Z. Walck, Inc. in 1964. Reprinted by permission of Robin Palmer.

"The Hulder-Maiden" from D'AULAIRES' TROLLS by Igri and Edgar Parin d'Aulaire. Copyright 1972 by Ingri and Edgar Parin d'Aulaire. Reprinted by permission of Doubleday and Company, Inc.

THE TROLL

Be wary of the loathsome troll
that slyly lies in wait
to drag you to his dingy hole
and put you on his plate.

His blood is black and boiling hot,
he gurgles ghastly groans.
He'll cook you in his dinner pot,
your skin, your flesh, your bones.

He'll catch your arms and clutch your legs
and grind you to a pulp,
then swallow you like scrambled eggs—
gobble! gobble! gulp!

So watch your steps when next you go
upon a pleasant stroll,
or you might end in the pit below
as supper for the troll.

Jack Prelutsky

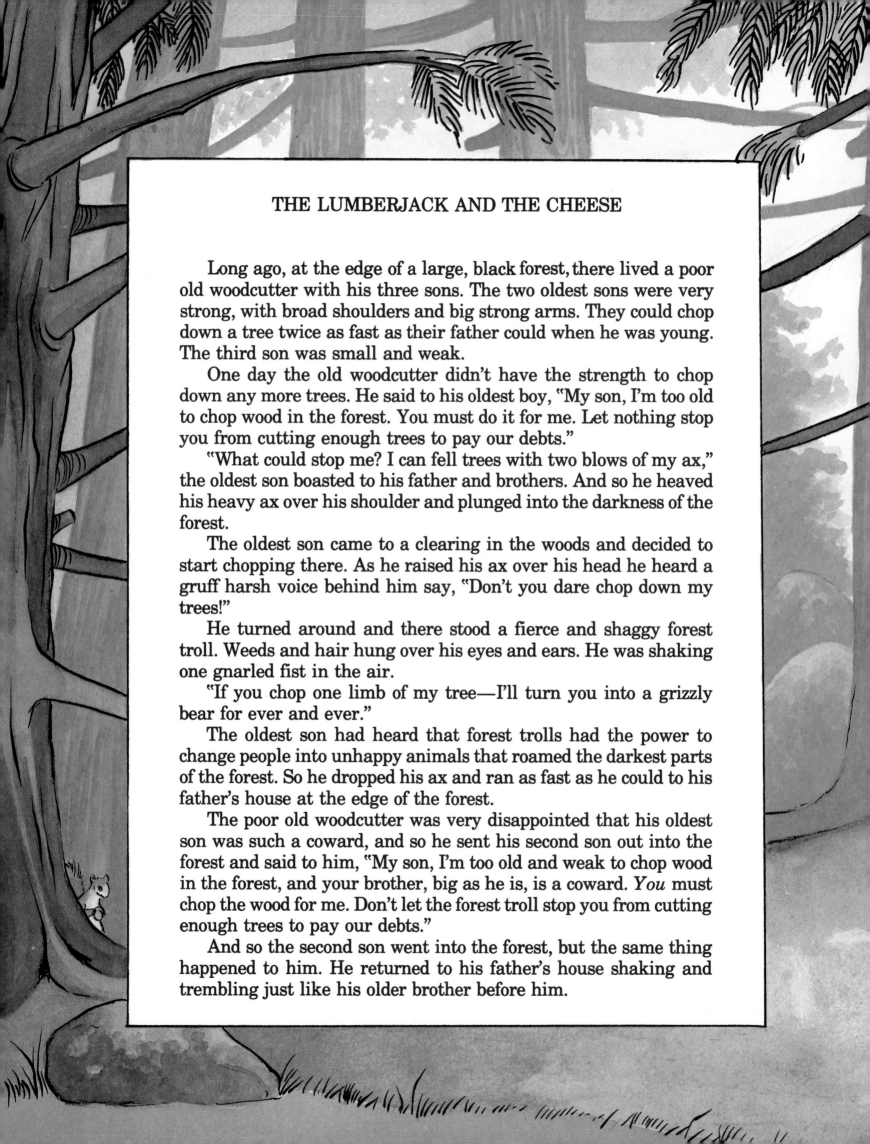

THE LUMBERJACK AND THE CHEESE

Long ago, at the edge of a large, black forest, there lived a poor old woodcutter with his three sons. The two oldest sons were very strong, with broad shoulders and big strong arms. They could chop down a tree twice as fast as their father could when he was young. The third son was small and weak.

One day the old woodcutter didn't have the strength to chop down any more trees. He said to his oldest boy, "My son, I'm too old to chop wood in the forest. You must do it for me. Let nothing stop you from cutting enough trees to pay our debts."

"What could stop me? I can fell trees with two blows of my ax," the oldest son boasted to his father and brothers. And so he heaved his heavy ax over his shoulder and plunged into the darkness of the forest.

The oldest son came to a clearing in the woods and decided to start chopping there. As he raised his ax over his head he heard a gruff harsh voice behind him say, "Don't you dare chop down my trees!"

He turned around and there stood a fierce and shaggy forest troll. Weeds and hair hung over his eyes and ears. He was shaking one gnarled fist in the air.

"If you chop one limb of my tree—I'll turn you into a grizzly bear for ever and ever."

The oldest son had heard that forest trolls had the power to change people into unhappy animals that roamed the darkest parts of the forest. So he dropped his ax and ran as fast as he could to his father's house at the edge of the forest.

The poor old woodcutter was very disappointed that his oldest son was such a coward, and so he sent his second son out into the forest and said to him, "My son, I'm too old and weak to chop wood in the forest, and your brother, big as he is, is a coward. *You* must chop the wood for me. Don't let the forest troll stop you from cutting enough trees to pay our debts."

And so the second son went into the forest, but the same thing happened to him. He returned to his father's house shaking and trembling just like his older brother before him.

The poor woodcutter was so disappointed that he started to weep. The woodcutter's youngest son put his arm on his father's shoulder and said, "Father, I will go into the forest and cut down enough trees to pay back all of our debts."

The woodcutter turned sadly to this son and said, "But you are half the size of your brothers—aren't you afraid of that selfish and evil forest troll?"

The big strong brothers laughed at their slender brother and asked, "How will you succeed against the troll if we could not?"

But the youngest son ignored their jeers. He quietly asked his father to let him take the cheese they had made that morning, and he wrapped it in his knapsack. With the knapsack slung around his neck and his ax over his shoulder—the youngest son plunged into the deep, dark forest.

Finally he came to the clearing where his older brothers had met the troll. There he placed his cheese on the ground next to a

tree. When he raised his ax above his head he heard the ugly troll's gruff voice, "Don't you dare chop down my tree."

The youngest son turned and quickly picked up his new white cheese and said, "If you forbid me to chop these trees I will squeeze the life from you the way I can squeeze the water from this white stone."

And the woodcutter's youngest son squeezed the fresh cheese until it turned to mush in his hand, and the whey dripped down and made a puddle at his feet.

The troll gasped with fear at the strength of this young boy.

"Oh no, young sir, I've never seen a human with such great strength. You may cut down as many trees as you wish."

Then the young boy replied, "No, troll, *you* cut down enough trees to fill a cart so I can bring them home to help pay my father's debts."

"Very well," said the troll, and he went to get his special ax that can cut trees faster than any woodcutter's son.

Just then, the youngest son spied the troll's pile of silver and gold behind the trees. He had heard that forest trolls hoarded their money, and he thought to himself, "*This* is why the troll guards his forest so fiercely."

And when the forest troll returned with his ax, the youngest son said, "Troll, you need only cut down enough trees to fill half a cart. The other half you must fill with gold and silver."

The forest troll gnashed his teeth and began to grumble, but the youngest son nimbly picked up a white stone nearby and cried, "Alright then, I'll squeeze the life from you!"

And the forest troll cringed and piled the cart high with gold and silver, and filled it with the biggest trees he could find.

Then the youngest son returned to his home with enough gold and silver to pay all his father's debts, and enough wood to keep them warm for many winters to come.

From then on the two brothers never made fun of the youngest son again, for the youngest son never told anyone how he tricked the great forest troll. And his brothers always wondered how their littlest brother had succeeded where they had failed.

TROLL SAT ALONE

from *The Fellowship of the Ring*
by J.R.R. Tolkien

Troll sat alone on his seat of stone,
And munched and mumbled a bare old bone;
   For many a year he had gnawed it near,
     For meat was hard to come by.
         Done by! Gum by!
In a cave in the hills he dwelt alone,
     And meat was hard to come by.

Up came Tom with his big boots on.
Said he to Troll: "Pray, what is yon?
   For it looks like the shin o' my nuncle Tim,
     As should be a-lyin' in graveyard.
         Caveyard! Paveyard!
This many a year has Tim been gone,
And I thought he were lyin' in graveyard."

"My lad," said Troll, "this bone I stole.
But what be bones that lie in a hole?
  Thy nuncle was dead as a lump o' lead,
    Afore I found his shinbone.
        Tinbone! Thinbone!
  He can spare a share for a poor old troll,
    For he don't need his shinbone."

Said Tom: "I don't see why the likes o' thee
Without axin' leave should go makin' free
  With the shank or the shin o' my father's kin;
    So hand the old bone over!
        Rover! Trover!
  Though dead he be, it belongs to he;
    So hand the old bone over!"

"For a couple o' pins," says Troll, and grins,
"I'll eat thee too, and gnaw thy shins.
    A bit o' fresh meat will go down sweet!
    I'll try my teeth on thee now.
            Hee now! See now!
I'm tired o' gnawing old bones and skins;
    I've a mind to dine on thee now."

But just as he thought his dinner was caught,
He found his hands had hold of naught.
    Before he could mind, Tom slipped behind
    And gave him the boot to larn him.
            Warn him! Darn him!
A bump o' the boot on the seat, Tom thought,
    Would be the way to larn him.

But harder than stone is the flesh and bone
Of a troll that sits in the hills alone.
  As well set your boot to the mountain's root,
    For the seat of a troll don't feel it.
        Peel it! Heal it!
  Old Troll laughed, when he heard Tom groan,
    And he knew his toes could feel it.

Tom's leg is game, since home he came,
And his bootless foot is lasting lame;
  But Troll don't care, and he's still there
    With the bone he boned from its owner.
        Doner! Boner!
  Troll's old seat is still the same,
    And the bone he boned from its owner!

THE TROLL'S INVITATION

by Robin Palmer & Pelagie Doane

In Gotland lies a high mound known by the name of Hoberg,
and within it, for many years, there lived a powerful troll. He was
as ugly as most of his brothers but not so large as many of them,
being about the size of a small man. Nevertheless he had the phe-
nomenal appetite for which trolls are famous. He could eat a sheep
for his lunch and come back for a whole cow for supper, topping it
off with a basket of peaches as well as bread and cheese. Since he
provided his own food, no one had any objection to the quantity of it.
In fact, the people in the neighborhood were only too happy that he
confined himself to this sort of meal and did not seem inclined to
stew up the baker's wife or the schoolmaster, as other trolls had
been known to do.

Nils, the farmer who plowed the land around Hoberg, always
treated the troll with the greatest courtesy, and was careful not to
touch the mound lest his digging cause a leak in the troll's roof.
Many a troll would have ignored this kindness or considered it his
just right, but the old man of Hoberg was friendly with his human
neighbors. He never played tricks on Nils and he sometimes gave
him a net full of fresh fish, so the two got on well together. The farm
prospered and Nils was a happy man.

12

One morning, however, the shepherd boy saw the farmer pacing up and down the barnyard with a troubled scowl on his face.

"That's a curious thing," thought the boy. "It is only a few days since my mistress had a son, her first child. This is surely a time of all others that the master should be rejoicing."

He therefore approached the farmer and asked him if anything had gone wrong. "One might think from the look on your face that the crops had failed," said the boy, whose name was Halvor, "but the farm has never been better. Do let me know whether I can help you."

The farmer was well aware that Halvor was a quick-witted lad, so he decided that it might be wise to tell him what the difficulty was. "It is true," said he, "that I should be the happiest of men, but I have a great problem. You know that the old troll of Hoberg has lived here for many years, and I have always been able to keep on good terms with him. Now we are planning a christening party for the baby, and a grand party it will be. But what about the troll? If I invite him, he will eat me out of house and home, and he may terrify my guests. On the other hand, if I do not invite him, he will be very angry. He might even bring ruin upon my farm."

Halvor was silent for a moment or two, thinking the matter over. Then he said, "You must certainly invite the troll, but in such a way that he will refuse the invitation."

"A fine idea," Nils replied, "if I knew how it could be done."

"Let me invite him," said the boy. "When I see him, I may know better what to say."

The farmer consented, and Halvor set out that afternoon to pay a visit to Hoberg. He found the troll's front door in the side of the hill and thumped boldly upon it. Immediately the troll flung it open.

"Dear me, dear me, what a racket!" he said. "A loud knock is most unpleasant to my ears."

"And surely his ears are the largest I have ever seen," thought the boy, "and his eyebrows are very bushy and fierce; but the eyes under them do not look unkind." So he spoke to the troll fearlessly.

"I am sorry my knock was so loud," said he. "My master, Nils, has sent me to bring you his greetings and to invite you to a christening party. Perhaps you have heard that he is the father of a fine baby boy."

"I had heard of it," the troll replied, "and I am pleased indeed that he has invited me. Tell him that I shall be very glad to come. No one has ever invited me to a christening before, but I have been told that they are fine affairs. I believe it is the custom to send a present to the baby."

"Most of the guests do give something," Halvor answered.

"Come in then," said the troll. "I see that you are carrying a basket and I shall put something into it."

With that he led the boy into his kitchen, a large room in the hillside, plainly furnished with oaken chairs and table like any other kitchen. From a closet at the back the troll pulled out a sack, just as you might pull out a sack of potatoes, and thrust a quart measure into it. When he drew it out, the measure was filled with gold.

Halvor's eyes opened wide in amazement as the gold was poured into his basket.

"Do you think that will be a good present?" asked the troll. "You must tell me, since I have never been invited before. Is this what people give?"

The boy wanted to do as well as possible for his master, so he answered, "That will do very well. Many give more, but some give less."

"Then I must add to it," said the troll. And once again he plunged his arm into the sack and filled the measure. "Is that better?"

"That is *much* better," Halvor replied. "Some give more, but many give less."

At that the troll scooped out so much gold that the basket was filled, and the boy realized it would be all he could do to carry it home. "Ah," said he, "I am sure none give more, and most give less."

"Good," replied the troll. "It sounds as if there might be some very important people at the christening. Who else is to be invited?"

Now Halvor knew that trolls are not fond of churchmen, so he answered, "I believe the bishop is one."

"The bishop," repeated the troll. "I am sorry to hear that. However, he is a man who carries his nose in the air. If I stay at the back, he is not likely to notice me. Who else is coming?"

Halvor thought he really must do something to prevent the troll from making his appearance, so this time he said, "I think my master is going to invite St. Peter."

"You don't mean it?" cried the troll. "I never would have thought your master had such high connections. I don't believe St. Peter and I would hit it off well at all. However, he is most unlikely to eat anything. I shall just stay in the dining room and keep out of his way."

"The dining room," thought Halvor, "that is the very place my master would like you to avoid." He wondered what on earth he could say that would discourage the old man. Then he remembered how the troll had objected to his thumping on the door, and he had a bright idea.

"My master has also planned to have very fine music," he said. "He is asking a band to come from the city, a band with six drummers."

When he heard that, the troll shook his head until his great ears flapped against it. "Oh no," he said. "No, no, that would be more than I could bear. I am dreadfully sorry, but you must please tell your master that I shall not be able to come. I should like to very much, but six drummers! You have no idea what a sound like that does to my head. It's worse than thunder and church bells. Thank him for his invitation, but really, I cannot accept it."

Halvor promised to give his master the message, and trudged back to the farm carrying his heavy burden. The farmer, you may be sure, was pleased at the way Halvor had solved the problem and gave him a gold piece for himself.

AS I WAS GOING UP AND DOWN

As I was going up and down,
I met a little troll,
He pulled my nose, and with two blows
I knocked him in a hole.

THE TERRIBLE TROLL

Once there was a king who loved his only daughter very much, but wished he had a son as well. Just when his daughter was old enough that he looked forward to a grandson, the King was told by a prophet that his own daughter's son would kill him. This news so terrified him that he determined never to let his daughter be married, for it was better to have no grandson at all than to be killed by his daughter's child.

The King called together all of his workmen and had them dig a deep round hole in the earth. Then he had a prison of brass built in the hole. When it was finished, he locked up his beautiful daughter so no man would ever see her. She would never again look upon the fields and the sea, only the sky and the sun, for there was a wide open window in the roof of the house of brass that she might breathe.

Time passed, and word of the prison in the earth spread throughout the kingdom. Handsome young men and princes from other lands came to the window and tried to catch glimpses of the prisoner. Great performances of strength and valor were held by the window, in hopes of winning the Princess's attention. When the King found out, he was angry and afraid, yet cowardly as he was, he had not quite the heart to kill the Princess, so he had her put in a huge brass-bound chest and thrust out to sea, that she might either be drowned or starved, or perhaps come to a country where she would be out of his way.

So the Princess floated and drifted in the chest on the sea all day and all night, but she was not afraid, so glad was she to be free from the brass prison.

When daylight came at last, the great chest was driven by the waves against the shore of an island. There the chest lay until a man of that country came and saw it, dragged it to the beach, and broke it open. Before his astonished eyes was a beautiful Princess. The man brought the Princess home and cared for her tenderly, and in a short time, the Princess agreed to be his bride.

Soon after, she gave birth to a son named Sven, but before he was born, the kind man died. However, the Princess was not alone for long, since word of her mysterious arrival had made her the center of attention. The young King of her new land asked her to marry him, promising to be a good father to her son.

As years passed, Sven came to his full strength, but the King was never pleased to have him around. The Princess and the King had a family of their own, but the first son, more handsome, strong and noble than the other children, was the son of another man, and not the King's favorite.

So the King thought of a plan to get rid of the boy. A great birthday party was planned for the Princess, who was beloved throughout the Kingdom, and the King announced that all of his subjects must present her with fine gifts—like gold cups, necklaces of amber, and beautiful horses. Only those with wonderful presents could attend.

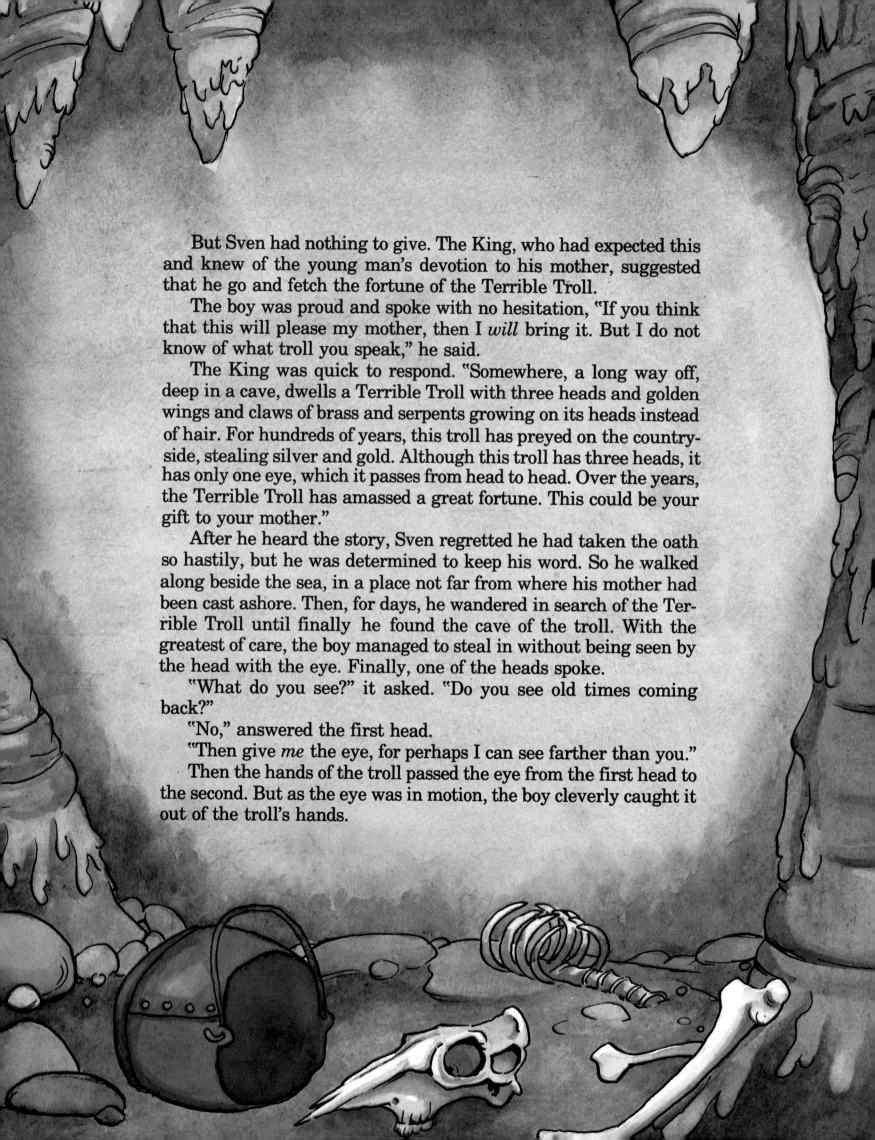

But Sven had nothing to give. The King, who had expected this and knew of the young man's devotion to his mother, suggested that he go and fetch the fortune of the Terrible Troll.

The boy was proud and spoke with no hesitation, "If you think that this will please my mother, then I *will* bring it. But I do not know of what troll you speak," he said.

The King was quick to respond. "Somewhere, a long way off, deep in a cave, dwells a Terrible Troll with three heads and golden wings and claws of brass and serpents growing on its heads instead of hair. For hundreds of years, this troll has preyed on the countryside, stealing silver and gold. Although this troll has three heads, it has only one eye, which it passes from head to head. Over the years, the Terrible Troll has amassed a great fortune. This could be your gift to your mother."

After he heard the story, Sven regretted he had taken the oath so hastily, but he was determined to keep his word. So he walked along beside the sea, in a place not far from where his mother had been cast ashore. Then, for days, he wandered in search of the Terrible Troll until finally he found the cave of the troll. With the greatest of care, the boy managed to steal in without being seen by the head with the eye. Finally, one of the heads spoke.

"What do you see?" it asked. "Do you see old times coming back?"

"No," answered the first head.

"Then give *me* the eye, for perhaps I can see farther than you."

Then the hands of the troll passed the eye from the first head to the second. But as the eye was in motion, the boy cleverly caught it out of the troll's hands.

"Where is the eye?" the second head shouted.

"You have it already," the first answered impatiently.

"Have you lost the eye, you fools? Have you lost it?" screeched the third head. "Shall we never see again? Shall we never see old times coming back?"

Then Sven slipped from behind them out of the cave and laughed aloud. "You'll never see anything again!" he cried.

When the troll heard this, it began to wail, "A stranger has stolen the eye. Please give it back!"

Sven could not help feeling sorry for it, whining so pitifully, so he agreed he would return the eye, in exchange for all of the silver and gold the troll had hoarded. First the troll refused, but in only a few moments it became so desperate that it told the boy where the treasure was hidden.

Sven knew he could not return the eye until he was safely gone with the fortune, so he kept the eye while he loaded up a sack. Then, when he was quite a distance from the cave, he called in a loud voice, "The eye is straight ahead. Walk very slowly and you will find it." And he ran as quickly as he could with so heavy a load.

But before he dropped the eye, Sven peeked through it, and what he saw was very strange. All that was light became dark, and all that was dark appeared light. The troll looked meek and gentle, and even quite handsome. Then Sven understood that trolls have troll-splinters in their eyes, and everything they see looks opposite. It is these troll-splinters that make the troll feel noble when it steals and happy when it causes pain, and attracts it to all that is gross and ugly.

Now that he was far from the terrible creature, Sven headed home. But he became confused and lost his way, and happened upon another kingdom, where the King was holding games and giving prizes to the best runners, boxers, and quoit-throwers. He decided to try his strength with the rest, but he threw the quoit so far that it went beyond what had ever been thrown before, and fell in the crowd, striking a man so hard that he died. Now this man was none other than the father of his mother, who had fled his own kingdom for fear his daughter had survived and had given birth to a son who should find him and kill him after all. Thus the King was destroyed by his own cowardice and by chance, and the prophecy was fulfilled.

Sven returned home with the fortune and was given a hero's welcome. The King, seeing the Princess's grief from the long absence of her son, had repented. A grand party was held and there was rejoicing throughout the kingdom.

THE HULDER-MAIDEN

by Ingri and Edgar Parin d'Aulaire

In the old days, when only narrow, twisting paths wound their way through the moss-grown mountains of Norway, few human beings ever set foot there. The mountains belonged to the trolls, who were as old and moss-grown as the mountains themselves.

When a child did grow up in these times, he had to beware of the hulder-maidens. For the dream of every hulder-maiden was to get a human boy in her power and have him for her husband. When a young man heard an enticing song and saw a beautiful girl leading a herd of small black cows on the lonely highlands, he had better make sure that one of the cowtails did not belong to her. If it did, he had better take to his heels, for if he let the hulder-maiden come too close, her beauty would bewitch him and he might follow her into her underground world. When that happened, trolls watching from afar opened their huge mouths wide as barn doors and laughed: "Haaa! That fellow will never be seen again."

Lucky was the young man who kept his head and brought the hulder-maiden home to his people. For when he took her to church and married her, a strange thing happened: The moment the church bells rang over her head, her tail dropped off and she gained an eternal soul like her husband's. Her trusted bridesmaid would quickly hide the tail so none of the wedding guests would spot it lying on the church steps.

Angrily the mountain trolls banged their stone doors to drown out the sound of the church bells. They were furious that one of their kin had gone astray.

But the hulder-people had no troll-splinters in their eyes and they were happy that one of their daughters had gained herself a soul. They saw to it that her husband prospered. As long as he treated his wife kindly, his barn was filled with hay and his cows grew sleek and fat.

The gnome who lived up in the hayloft helped too, for the hulder-bride well knew that the bristling whiskers and glowing amber eyes in the far corner of the barn did not belong to a cat. Whenever she milked, she set aside a saucer for the gray-clad gnome, and on holy evenings she gave him his share of the pudding. In return, the gnome would run to unfriendly neighbors' barns and whisk away an armful of hay whenever he thought the cows looked hungry.

The hulder-maiden's fairy beauty soon faded, but she made a good wife. She was husky and strong and bore her husband fine children. Her children were proud of having a hulder-mother, for that made them different from other people. They could see and hear things that were hidden from others. Some of them even understood the language of the birds and the beasts, and they became great storytellers. Even trolls came to listen and sat spellbound all through the night when the hulder-children told their strange tales. Neither trolls nor troll-hags had power over them, so they were not afraid. But they had no love for the uncouth creatures.

Late one night a hulder-lad said to a troll and his hag: "Now I shall tell you the story of the very first trolls, the fearsome frost giants.

"They lived in castles of ice, surrounded by shimmering fences of northern lights. They were as wild as the mountains themselves and pelted the valleys with snow and ice—nobody dared to live in a place near them. They had more gold and silver than they knew what to do with, and hard-working gnomes were forever bringing them more. So when they were in a good mood, they would playfully toss huge balls of gold to each other. The frost giants were much bigger and stronger than you plain trolls, and some of them had as many as five hundred heads on their shoulders. What trolls they were!"

"Tell us more," said the trolls, their mouths agape.

"Then churches were built down in the valleys and the fine pealing of the bells hurt their rough ears so badly that they took their vast treasures and moved into the mountains."

"What then, what then?" cried the trolls, and quite forgot to look out for the rising sun.

"Well," said the boy, "don't you know that yourselves? By and by the giants faded into the past and trolls like you took over their mountain halls. You think you have all their treasures, but you are paupers compared to them. The biggest ball of gold they hid behind the mountain yonder."

"Where?" cried the trolls, and spun around. They stared straight into the golden eye of the rising sun.

With a loud crack they burst and turned to stone. One became a mountain, the other a heap of rubble. They had done what no troll must ever do. For trolls were creatures of darkness and just one glance at the sun was enough to destroy them.

Many trolls must have been tricked in this way, for none have been seen walking around for over a hundred years. Have they all burst or are some still hiding behind their stone doors?

Are the gnomes still mining deep in the mountains?

And are the hulder-people still herding their fat little cows down under the hills? We cannot be certain.

But we do know that every time a troll burst, the splinter in his eye was scattered far and wide. Maybe that is why there are people everywhere today who see things askew. What is bad looks good to them and what is wrong looks right. They do not know that they have troll-splinters in their eyes and you cannot see them. But you can be very sure that the troll-splinters are there.